My First Animal Library

Raccoons

by Martha E. H. Rustad

Bullfrog Books

Ideas for Parents and Teachers

Bullfrog Books give children practice reading nonfiction at the earliest levels. Repetition, familiar words, and photos support early readers.

Before Reading
- Discuss the cover photo. What does it tell them?
- Look at the picture glossary together. Read and discuss the words.

Read the Book
- "Walk" through the book and look at the photos. Let the child ask questions. Point out the photo labels.
- Read the book to the child, or have him or her read independently.

After Reading
- Prompt the child to think more. Ask: Have you ever seen a raccoon? What was it doing?

Bullfrog Books are published by Jump!
5357 Penn Avenue South
Minneapolis, MN 55419
www.jumplibrary.com

Library of Congress Cataloging-in-Publication Data
Rustad, Martha E. H. (Martha Elizabeth Hillman), 1975-
   Raccoons / by Martha E.H. Rustad.
     p. cm. —(Bullfrog books. My first animal library, nocturnal animals)
   Summary: "This easy-to-read nonfiction story tells a "night in the life" of a raccoon family, from waking up, finding food and swimming, to going back to sleep when the sun comes up"—Provided by publisher.
   Audience: K to grade 3.
   Includes bibliographical references and index.
   ISBN 978-1-62031-072-4 (hardcover)
   ISBN 978-1-62496-072-7 (ebook)
   1. Raccoon—Juvenile literature. I. Title.
QL737.C26R87 2014
599.76'32--dc23
                                                2013004612

Series Editor: Rebecca Glaser
Series Designer: Ellen Huber
Book Designer: Lindaanne Donohoe

Photo Credits: Getty, 8, 10, 20–21; iStockPhoto, 11, 14–15, 18–19, 23bl, 23br; Shutterstock, cover, 1, 3 (both), 4, 5, 6, 7, 9, 12–13, 16 (raccoons), 19, 22, 23tl, 23bl, 24; Veer, 16 (food), 17

Printed in the United States of America at Corporate Graphics, in North Mankato, Minnesota.
4-2013 / PO 1003
10 9 8 7 6 5 4 3 2 1

Table of Contents

Raccoons at Night

The sun sets.

Night begins.

Raccoons wake up.

den

A raccoon climbs
down from her den.

She waddles to
a pond.

She grabs a crab.

Her fingers
open the shell.

fingers

Sharp teeth rip the food.

Her eyes see in the dark.

She catches fish and frogs.

She brings food to her babies.

The hungry kits wait in the den.

Their cozy home is in a tree.

Mom is back!

The kits come down.

They gobble up the snack.

Mom teaches the kits.

They learn to sniff for food.

They learn to swim.

Watch out! A fox!

Get back in the den.

The mother keeps
her kits safe.

The sun rises.

Day begins.

Raccoons go to sleep.

Parts of a Raccoon

eyes
Raccoons can see in the dark.

ears
Large ears help raccoons listen for danger.

tail
Stripes cover raccoons bushy tails.

nose
Raccoons have a strong sense of smell.

paws
Raccoon paws look like human hands.

Picture Glossary

den
A home for an animal; raccoons like to make dens in trees.

sniff
To smell; raccoons have a strong sense of smell.

kit
A young raccoon.

waddle
To walk with short, swaying steps.

Index

To Learn More

Learning more is as easy as 1, 2, 3.

1) Go to www.factsurfer.com

2) Enter "raccoons" into the search box.

3) Click the "Surf" button to see a list of websites.

With factsurfer.com, finding more information is just a click away.